P9-EEM-499

The
Story
of
Jesus

By

REV. LAWRENCE G. LOVASIK, S.V.D.
Divine Word Missionary

CATHOLIC BOOK PUBLISHING CO.
NEW YORK

TO THE READER . . .

VATICAN Council II stated: "It is common knowledge that among all the Scriptures, even those of the New Testament the gospels have a special preeminence, and rightly so, for they are the principal witness for the life and teaching of the Incarnate Word, our Savior" (*Divine Revelation,* no. 18).

The purpose of THE STORY OF JESUS is to help you to know and love Jesus Christ still more. No subject should be dearer to you than the adorable Person of Jesus Christ, the Divine Word Incarnate, and none can be more useful for your salvation.

You have everything in Christ, and without Him neither salvation nor sanctification is possible. Through Him every grace is given to us and all glory rendered to His Father.

The beautiful pictures in living color will make His story even more appealing.

Fr. Lawrence S.V.D.

NIHIL OBSTAT: Daniel V. Flynn, J.C.D. — *Censor Librorum*
IMPRIMATUR: Joseph T. O'Keefe — *Vicar General,*
Archdiocese of New York

(T-535)

INDEX

Jesus' Birth Is Announced to Mary

THE Angel Gabriel said to Mary: "Hail, full of grace, the Lord is with you. Blessed are you among women." Mary was troubled and wondered about this greeting. The angel then said: "The Holy Spirit will come upon you."

The Angel continued: "Do not be afraid, Mary, for you have found grace with God. Behold, you shall conceive in your womb and shall bring forth a Son; and you shall call His name Jesus."

After learning that this was to be done by the power of God, Mary said: "I am the servant of the Lord. Let it be done to me as you say."

Mary Visits Her Cousin Elizabeth

MARY hurried off to the hill country to visit Elizabeth. When Elizabeth heard Mary's greeting, the baby moved within her and she said to Mary: "Blest are you among women and blest is the fruit of your womb. Who am I that the mother of the Lord should come to me?"

Mary replied: "My being proclaims the greatness of the Lord, my spirit finds joy in God my Savior. All ages to come shall call me blessed. God Who is mighty has done great things for me."

Mary stayed with Elizabeth for three months and then returned home to Nazareth.

Jesus Is Born

THE Roman Emperor Augustus ordered all the people under his rule to be counted. Joseph and Mary left their home in Nazareth and traveled to Bethlehem.

So many people had come to be registered that there was no room for them in the inn. Outside the town, on the hills, they found a cave. Here Jesus was born. Mary wrapped Him in soft clothes and laid Him in a manger."

Nearby, shepherds were watching their sheep. Suddenly an angel appeared and said: "Do not be afraid, for behold, I bring you good news of great joy, for today in the town of Bethlehem a Savior has been born. You will find the infant Jesus lying in a manger."

Other angels appeared. They praised God, saying: "Glory to God in high heaven, peace on earth to those on whom His favor rests."

The shepherds hurried off and found Mary and Joseph, and saw the Baby lying in the manger. When the shepherds saw Him they told them what the angel had said about this Child. The shepherds went back, singing praises to God for all they had heard and seen.

Simeon Foretells Jesus' Mission

WHEN Jesus was forty days old, Joseph and Mary carried Him to the Temple to offer Him to God as the Law required.

Simeon had been told by the Holy Spirit that he would not die before he had seen the Lord's Messiah. Simeon took the Child Jesus in his arms, and gave thanks to God. He told Mary that she would have to suffer many things because she loved Jesus.

The Three Wise Men Come to Worship Jesus

WHEN Jesus was still a baby, three Wise Men came from a far land to Jerusalem. They had seen a star in the East and had come to adore the newborn King. Herod, the ruler, feared this new King, so he told the Wise Men to find the new King and report to him.

The star went ahead of them until it came over the place where the Child was. They went into the house and saw the Child with His mother Mary. They knelt down and worshiped Him: then they opened their bags and offered Him presents: gold, frankincense, and myrrh.

God warned them in a dream not to go back to Herod; so they went back to their country by another road.

7

Jesus Speaks with the Teachers

WHEN Jesus was twelve years old, He went up to Jerusalem with Mary and Joseph. After the feast, His parents started home and discovered that Jesus was not with them. For three days they looked for Him.

At last they found Jesus in the Temple, surrounded by learned men, listening to them and asking questions.

His mother said to Him: "Son, why have You done this to us?" He answered: "Why did you have to look for Me? Didn't you know that I had to be in My Father's house?"

Mary did not understand that Jesus was doing the work of His heavenly Father. He returned obediently to Nazareth.

Jesus Helps Joseph in the Shop

THE Holy Family at Nazareth lived a life of prayer and work. Jesus helped Joseph in the carpenter shop, and when Joseph died He supported His Mother until the age of thirty.

Jesus always showed respect, love, and obedience to His parents. He gave all boys and girls an example of how they must obey and love their parents.

The Gospel says that Jesus grew in wisdom and age and grace before God and men. He was getting ready for the work His Father gave Him to do as our Teacher and Redeemer.

The Holy Family is an example for all Christian families.

9

Jesus Begins His Father's Work

ONE day Jesus entered the synagogue, the place of worship in Nazareth. He told the people that He was the Messiah.

He had been sent by God the Father to preach the Gospel to the poor, to free the captives, to give sight to the blind, to deliver prisoners, and to preach the coming of the Lord.

They marveled at the beautiful words that He spoke. They said: "Isn't He the Son of Joseph?"

He said to them: "A prophet is never welcomed in his own home town."

The people did not believe Him. They became angry and chased Him from the synagogue, and even tried to kill Him. But Jesus walked away.

Jesus Chooses the Twelve Apostles

JESUS went up a mountain and remained in prayer all night with His Father. At daybreak He came down and selected twelve men. These were to share His life and be with Him always. They were to be called Apostles.

They were: Simon Peter and Andrew, James and John, Philip and Bartholomew (or Nathaniel), Matthew and Thomas, James and Simon, Jude Thaddeus and Judas (who betrayed Him).

Jesus chose these men to be the foundation of His Kingdom and His Church, because He was to give them the powers of the priesthood: to offer the sacrifice of the Mass, to forgive sins, and to teach in His name. They would take His place on earth and give their powers to other priests.

11

Jesus Cures Many Sick People

ONE day at sunset the people brought all their sick family and friends to Jesus. When our Lord saw the great crowd, He laid His hands on the sick among them and healed them.

Jesus came into the world to free us from sin and evil of every kind. He showed tender compassion for the sick and many times cured them of their illness.

Jesus said: "Come to Me, all of you who are tired from carrying your heavy loads, and I will give you rest. Take My yoke and put it on you, and learn from Me because I am gentle and humble in spirit; and you will find rest."

Jesus Speaks with Nicodemus

A RULER of the Jews, named Nicodemus, went to Jesus by night and said: "Teacher, we know that God sent You, for no one could work the miracles that You do unless God was with him."

Jesus told him that unless a man is born again by means of water and the Spirit (in Baptism,) he cannot enter the Kingdom of God. Jesus meant that no one can be a child of God without a new heart and spirit which only God can give.

Nicodemus believed in Jesus. He was born again and became a child of God.

Jesus Gives the Sermon on the Mount

ONE day Jesus went up the side of a hill, where all could see Him, and He began to teach the large crowd of people who had come to hear Him.

He said that God made us to know, love, and serve Him in this world, so that we can be happy forever with Him in heaven.

To be happy we must be poor in spirit; we must be meek; we must be sorry for our sins; we must be holy; we must be merciful; we must be pure; we must be peaceful, and willing to suffer for God.

Jesus said: "Be glad and happy, because a great reward is kept for you in heaven."

Jesus Teaches Trust in God

JESUS wants all people to know how good God is. He told His disciples to look at the birds of the air who do not sow, but God gives them their food.

He pointed to the lilies of the field which God made. They are more beautiful than the greatest king in his royal robes.

If we remember this lesson we will thank God for our home, our clothing, our food, because He has given us His love in wonderful ways.

Jesus said: "You are like light for the whole world. Your light must shine before people, so that they will see the good things you do and give praise to your Father in heaven."

15

Jesus Calls for Love of Neighbor

JESUS said: "Treat others the way you would have them treat you: this sums up the law and the prophets. Judge not and you will not be judged.

"When someone asks you for something, give it to him; when someone wants to borrow something, lend it to him."

He told the disciples that they must never say an unkind word about anyone, never do an unkind thing to anyone.

Whenever we forget what Jesus wants and we hurt anyone, we must tell him at once that we are sorry, then God will be pleased and He will hear our prayers.

Jesus Helps Peter Catch Many Fish

JESUS told Peter to row out to the middle of the lake to fish. Peter obeyed at once, although he had fished all night and caught nothing. He caught so many fish that his boat almost sank.

Peter knew that he was in the presence of the great power of God. He fell on his knees before Jesus and said: "Leave me, Lord; I am a sinful man."

Jesus said to Peter: "Do not be afraid, from now on you will catch men." Jesus invited the disciples to be fishers of men, and they left everything to follow Him.

Jesus teaches us that without His help we can do nothing. He gives us the grace to be good.

17

Jesus Cures a Crippled Person

JESUS came into His own town. Some men brought Him a man who was lying on a bed and unable to move.

Jesus saw the faith of those who carried the sick man, and so He said to the crippled man: "Take courage, son, your sins are forgiven you."

Then to show that He could forgive sins, Jesus said to the man: "Arise, take up your bed and go to your house." And the man arose. He was completely cured.

Through His priests Jesus now takes away our sins in the Sacrament of Penance if we are truly sorry for them.

Jesus Cures an Official's Son

THE son of a royal official was sick. His father went to Jesus and begged Him to come to his home and heal his son who was about to die.

Jesus said: "Unless you see miracles you do not believe." But the officer begged more earnestly, saying: "Lord, come to my home before my son dies."

As soon as our Lord said to the sad father: "Go to your home, your son lives," servants came to say the boy was cured at that very moment.

The father and his family believed in Jesus, for they had seen His power.   19

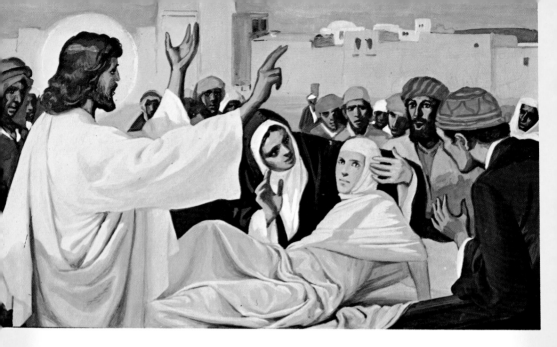

Jesus Raises a Widow's Son

WHEN Jesus came to the town of Naim with His disciples, they met a funeral procession. It was the funeral of the only son of a widow.

Seeing the mother's sorrow, Jesus was moved with pity. He told her not to cry. Then He said to the dead young man: "I say to you, arise."

The young man who was dead sat up and began to speak, and Jesus gave him to his mother. Everyone in Naim rejoiced and praised God.

They said: "A great prophet has risen among us! God has visited His people."

Jesus Cures a Blind Man

A BLIND man sat on the roadside. When he heard that Jesus was near, he cried: "Jesus, Son of David, have mercy on me." Jesus stopped and the blind man was brought to Him.

When the man came to Jesus, he cried out: "Lord, make me see." Jesus said: "Receive your sight, your faith has saved you."

The man could see again and went away praising the goodness of God.

We, too, are blind to the most wonderful things which our Faith offers us in its doctrine and sacraments. We should ask Jesus to let us see by faith the treasures we have in the Catholic Church.

21

Jesus Feeds Five Thousand People

A GREAT crowd of people listened to Jesus preaching most of the day. They were hungry and there was no place to buy food.

Jesus took into His hands five loaves and two fish which a boy had brought. He blessed them and told His Apostles to give them to the people.

The Apostles passed the bread and fish to everyone, as much as needed. Twelve baskets of food were left.

The people said: "Surely this is the Prophet Who was to come to the world!" They wanted to make Him King, but Jesus went off to the hills by Himself.

Jesus Calms a Storm at Sea

JESUS was tired. He asked His Apostles to row Him across a lake. Then He fell asleep.

Suddenly, a great storm arose, and the boat seemed to be sinking. The Apostles became frightened and wakened Jesus, saying, "Lord, save us! We are drowning."

Jesus stood up and said, "Peace, be still!" At once the wind stopped blowing, the waves quieted down, and there was a great calm.

Then Jesus said to the disciples: "Where is your faith?"

They said to one another, "Who is this Man? He gives orders to the winds and waves, and they obey Him!"

23

Jesus Promises the Eucharist

THE people followed Jesus to the other side of the shore. He told them they were only looking for more of the earthly bread He had given them. But He would give them the Bread from heaven.

"I am the living Bread which came down from heaven. If anyone eats this Bread, he will live forever. And the Bread that I will give is My own flesh for the life of the world.

"My Flesh is real food and My Blood is real drink."

Some followers of Jesus left because they could not believe Him.

Jesus Speaks of His Death and Resurrection

ONE day, Jesus said to His disciples: "The Son of Man is to be betrayed into the hands of men, and they will kill Him. Then on the third day He will rise again."

The disciples were very sad about this, but they did not understand. Yet they were afraid to ask Jesus about it.

On two other occasions Jesus told them about His Death and Resurrection.

At another time Jesus said: "The Son of Man will be handed over to the Gentiles, who will whip Him and kill Him, but on the third day He will rise to life."

25

Jesus Shows His Glory

PETER, James and John climbed a tall mountain with Jesus. There they saw Him as they had never seen Him before. His face shone as the sun. His clothes were white as snow.

Then the three disciples saw Moses and Elijah talking with Jesus. Peter said: "Lord, it is a good thing that we are here."

A voice from heaven said: "This is My beloved Son, listen to Him." Jesus told the Apostles not to fear.

When they climbed down the mountain, Jesus told them not to tell anyone what they had seen until after He had risen from the dead.

Jesus Hears His Mother Praised

ONCE a woman from the crowd called out to Jesus: "Blest is the womb that bore You and the breasts that nursed You!"

Jesus said to her: "Rather, blest are they who hear the word of God and keep it."

Jesus praised His Mother because no one ever obeyed God as she did. She welcomed the angel who told her that she was to be the Mother of God. She said: "I am the servant of the Lord. Let it be done to me as you say."

We, too, will be blessed by God if we do His holy will. Jesus once said: "If you love Me, keep My commandments."

27

Jesus Blesses Children

JESUS loved little children. One day while He was teaching the people, they were bringing their little children to Him that He might touch them.

The Apostles tried to keep the children away, because Jesus was tired.

But Jesus said: "Let the children come to Me. Do not hinder them. The Kingdom of God belongs to such as these. Unless you change and become like little children you will never enter the Kingdom of Heaven."

And He laid His hands on their heads and blessed them.

Jesus Gives Life to a Little Girl

A MAN named Jairus was waiting for Jesus. He knelt before Jesus and said: "My little daughter is dying. Please come and lay Your hand on her, that she may live."

Jesus followed him to his home and found all the people crying. They said the little girl was dead.

Jesus told the people: "Stop crying; she is not dead, but asleep."

Jesus went inside with the parents. Taking the girl's hand, He said: "Little girl, arise." The girl stood up and began to walk.

29

Jesus Cures a Leper

LEPROSY is a skin disease that is painful and terrible to look at. Lepers are kept away from other people.

A leper came up and bowed low in front of Jesus. "Lord," he said, "if You want to, You can cure me."

Jesus stretched out His hand, touched him and said, "I do want to cure you. Be cured!" And his leprosy was cured at once.

Jesus had pity on the sick. His example should teach us to be kind to our neighbor.

Leprosy is a skin disease. It reminds us of mortal sin, the greatest evil in the world. Jesus cleanses us from sin in the Sacrament of Penance.

Jesus Cures a Deaf-Mute

A MAN who could not hear or speak came to Jesus. Jesus put His fingers in the man's ears, then He touched the man's tongue and said: "Be opened."

At once the man could hear and speak clearly to Jesus and his friends.

All who watched Jesus cure this man were surprised, and they said: "He has done all things well; He has made both the deaf to hear and the dumb to speak."

Our ears should be open to hear the truths of eternal life. Our speech ought to be used to praise God.

31

Jesus with Martha and Mary

JESUS often visited Martha, her sister Mary, and their brother Lazarus. One day Mary sat at the feet of Jesus, listening to Him, while Martha rushed about preparing the meal.

Martha became annoyed and said: "Lord, is it no concern of Yours that my sister has left me to serve alone? Tell her therefore to help me."

Jesus replied: "Martha, Martha, you are anxious and troubled about many things; and yet only one thing is needful. Mary has chosen the best part, and it will not be taken away from her."

Jesus teaches us that only one thing is needful in this world and that is to possess God and save our soul.

Mary Washes the Feet of Jesus

SIX days before the Feast of the Passover Jesus came to the house of Lazarus and his sisters. They reclined at table and Martha served.

Mary took a pound of genuine ointment of great value and anointed the feet of Jesus. Then with her hair she dried them.

Judas Iscariot was very angry that she had not sold the ointment and given the money to the poor. Jesus said: "Leave her alone. She has done a beautiful thing for Me. You have the poor with you always, but you will not always have Me. When she poured this perfume on My body, she was preparing it for My burial."

Jesus Weeps over the City

JESUS went out to the Mount of Olives with His disciples. He wept over Jerusalem. He said: "O Jerusalem, Jerusalem! You murder the prophets and stone the messengers that are sent to you. How often have I longed to gather your children round Me like a bird gathering her little ones under her wings, and you would never have it."

Then He spoke of the Temple buildings. "I tell you every stone will be thrown down till there is not a single one left standing upon another."

Jesus proclaimed the downfall of Jerusalem which was to murder even God's own Son.

Thirty-five years later Jerusalem was destroyed by the Roman Army.

Jesus Enters Jerusalem in Triumph

JESUS started for Jerusalem once more. On the way the Apostles brought a donkey. They put their cloaks over her back, and Jesus rode on the donkey into Jerusalem.

Great crowds of people went with Jesus. Some threw their cloaks on the road. Some cut branches from the trees and spread them in His path. All the people shouted: "Blessed is He who comes as King in the name of the Lord!"

This made the enemies of Jesus angry, and they decided to kill Him.

This entry into Jerusalem was a sign of Jesus's desire to rule over the souls of all people as King.

35

Jesus Gives Us the Eucharist

JESUS knew that He would soon be put to death. So He told the Apostles to meet Him in a certain room for His Last Supper with them.

Jesus took some bread, and when He had said the blessing, He broke it and gave it to the disciples. "Take it and eat," He said, "this is My Body."

Then He took a cup, and when He had returned thanks He gave it to them. "Drink, all of you, from this," He said, "for this is My Blood, the Blood of the new Covenant, which is to be poured out for many for the forgiveness of sins. Do this as a remembrance of Me."

Jesus gave His Apostles His greatest Gift— His own Body and Blood under the appearances of bread and wine. He made the Apostles priests and gave them the power to do the same thing in memory of Him.

Jesus Speaks about Heaven to the Apostles

AFTER the Last Supper, Jesus continued to talk with the Apostles. He knew that He was going to leave them by His Death. So He gave them words of hope about heaven and their future life.

"Do not let your hearts be troubled. Have faith in God and faith in Me. There are many rooms in My Father's house.

"I am now going to prepare a place for you, and after I have gone and prepared a place, I will come back to take you with Me.

"I give you a new commandment: love one another. As I have loved you, so you must love one another. By your love for one another, everyone will know that you are My disciples."

Jesus Promises to Send the Holy Spirit

JESUS then went on to speak of the Holy Spirit and the work He would do in His Church.

"I shall ask the Father, and He will give you another Advocate to be with you forever, the Spirit of Truth Whom the world can never receive since it neither sees nor knows Him. But you know Him, because He is with you, He is in you.

"The Paraclete, the Holy Spirit, Whom the Father will send in My name, will teach you everything and remind you of all that I told you Myself."

Then Jesus prayed to His heavenly Father for Himself and for His disciples and for all who would believe in Him.

39

Jesus in His Agony

JESUS went with His disciples into the Garden of Gethsemane.

Kneeling down, He began to pray: "Father, if You are willing, remove this cup from Me. Yet not My will but Yours be done." And there appeared an Angel from heaven to strengthen

40 Him.

Jesus Is Betrayed by Judas

JUDAS, followed by a crowd with swords and clubs, approached Jesus. Judas had told them: "Whomever I kiss, that is He; lay hold of Him."

As Judas drew near, Jesus said to him: "Judas, do you betray the Son of Man with a kiss?" Judas went straight up to Him and said: "Hail, Rabbi!" and kissed Him.

One of those with Jesus cut off the ear of the servant of the high priest with a sword. Jesus cured the wound and told him to put the sword away. "Those who use the sword," He said, "are sooner or later destroyed by it." Then the crowd took Jesus and led Him away to the high priest.

Jesus Declares He Is the Son of God

JESUS was questioned by the high priest and Council of Elders who were trying to find an accusation against Him. Finally, the high priest said: "By the living God, tell us if You are the Messiah, the Son of God."

Jesus replied: "I am. And I tell you that you will see the Son of Man seated at the right hand of the Power and coming on the clouds of heaven."

The high priest cried out: "He has blasphemed." So he tore his clothes and exclaimed: "What is your opinion?" They all answered: "He deserves to die."

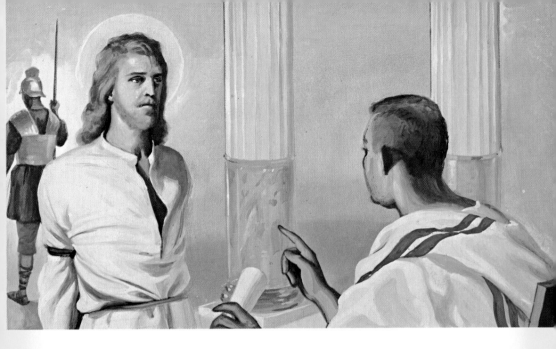

Jesus Is Brought before Pilate

THE high priest and the Council sent Jesus to the Roman governor. Pilate asked Jesus: "Are You the King of the Jews?"

Jesus replied: "I am a King. That is why I was born, and why I have come into the world, to bear witness to the truth."

The chief priests and elders accused Jesus, but He made no answer. Pilate wondered. Finally, he said to the people: "I find no guilt in Him."

"We will bear the blame," shouted the people. "His blood be upon us and upon our children!"

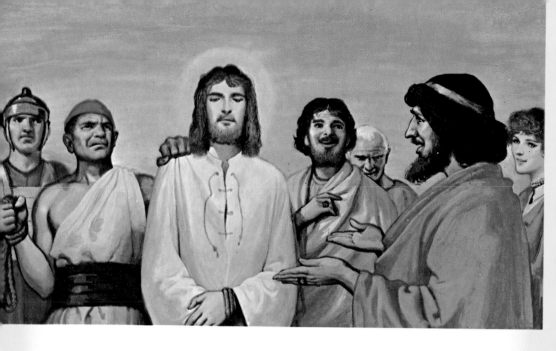

Jesus Is Mocked by Herod

WHILE Pilate was trying to decide what to do about Jesus, he learned that He was from Galilee. So he sent Him to Herod, the ruler of Galilee, who happened to be in Jerusalem.

Herod was very pleased to see Jesus because he wanted to have Him work some miracle. But Jesus would not even speak to Herod.

Herod and his guards then treated Jesus with contempt and insults. They then placed a bright robe on Him and sent Him back to Pilate.

Jesus Is Scourged by the Soldiers

PILATE gave Jesus into the hands of the Roman soldiers to be scourged. The soldiers stripped Jesus of His garments and beat Him with rods till His body was covered with blood.

Jesus Is Crowned with Thorns

THE soldiers placed a crown of thorns on Jesus' head and threw over Him a purple robe—the color of kings. Placing a reed in His right hand, they bowed down before Him and cried out: "Hail, King of the Jews!"

They mocked Him, spat upon Him and, taking a reed, they struck Him on the head.

Jesus Is Condemned to Death

PILATE brought Jesus out to the people with the crown of thorns and the purple robe upon Him.

Pilate said: "Behold the Man! I bring Him out to you that you may know that I find no guilt in Him." When the chief priests and attendants saw Jesus, they cried out: "Crucify Him!"

Then Pilate washed his hands before the Jews, saying, "I am innocent of the blood of this just Man." And he gave Jesus into the hands of the soldiers to be crucified.

Jesus Consoles Some Women

THE Roman soldiers laid the Cross on Jesus, and then started for Calvary—the place of the crucifixion. Jesus fell under the weight of the Cross. The soldiers forced Simon of Cyrene to help Him.

A great crowd of people was following Jesus. Jesus said: "Daughters of Jerusalem, do not weep for Me, but weep for yourselves and your children."

When they reached Calvary, they stretched Jesus out upon the Cross. With heavy nails they nailed His hands and feet to the wooden beams. They raised the Cross and set it in the hole which they had dug.

Jesus Dies on the Cross

JESUS prayed: "Father, forgive them; they do not know what they are doing."

Seeing His Mother there with the disciple whom He loved, Jesus said to His Mother, "Woman, there is your son." And to John He said: "There is your mother." Jesus gave us His Mother as His death-bed gift of love.

Then, with a loud voice, Jesus prayed: "Father, into Your hands I place my spirit." Having said this, He died. The earth shook, rocks split, tombs were opened and the curtain of the Temple was torn in two.

The Side of Jesus Is Pierced

ONE of the soldiers plunged his spear into the side of Jesus, and at once blood and water poured out. Seeing what had happened, he said: "Surely this was a just Man."

Jesus poured out the last drop of His Blood for our salvation. His Heart is a sign of His love for us. That Heart was pierced—it is always open to receive us when we have sinned.

By His death Jesus won life for us and made up for our sins. We must hate sin and use our life for Jesus.

Jesus Is Taken Down and Buried

NICODEMUS and Joseph of Arimathea were rulers of the Jews and friends of Jesus. After obtaining permission from Pilate, they came with their friends and took down the body of Jesus.

They put the broken body of Jesus into Mary's waiting arms. She felt pain and love, love of Jesus and love of us. She gave her Son for our salvation.

Wrapping it in fine linen and precious spices, they placed the body of Jesus in Joseph's new tomb.

They placed a great stone at the entrance of the cave. The rulers of the Jews posted a guard of soldiers at the tomb.

Jesus Rises from the Dead

ON three occasions Jesus had told His Apostles that He would rise on the third day after His death.

At dawn on Sunday morning, all at once the earth began to tremble, and in some places great cracks opened in the ground. While the earth quaked, a mighty angel of the Lord came down from heaven and rolled away the stone and sat upon it. In their terror the watchmen fell to the ground like dead men.

When they revived, they saw that the grave was open and empty. Then they ran to the city of Jerusalem, to tell the chief priests and Pharisees about the angel and the earthquake and the empty tomb.

Jesus rose by His own power, a glorious Victor, as His wounds sparkled like jewels. Death and sin were conquered.

The Divinity shone forth through the glorified Body of Jesus, and joy poured into His Soul. He appeared to His friends to make them share in the joy of His victory. He surely appeared to His Mother first.

The Resurrection of Jesus proves that He is the Son of God and that His teaching is true. It is His greatest miracle.

An Angel Announces the Resurrection

EARLY in the morning, Mary Magdalene and some other women carried spices to the tomb to anoint the body of Jesus. They were wondering who would roll back the heavy stone from the tomb.

When they arrived there, they were very much surprised to see the stone rolled back and an Angel standing before them. The Angel said: "He is not here, for He has risen, as He said He would!"

He told them not to be afraid, but to go tell Peter and others that Jesus had risen from the dead, and that He would see them again.

Peter and John Visit the Empty Tomb

WHEN Peter and John heard the story, they had to go and see for themselves. They ran to the tomb and went inside.

They saw the linen cloths that had covered the body of Jesus and the cloth that had been around His head. But His body was not there.

The two Apostles went outside and thought about what they had seen. They went back to tell the other disciples what they had found.

Jesus also appeared to Mary Magdalene and said to her: "Do not cling to Me, because I have not yet ascended to the Father. But go and find the brothers, and tell them: I am ascending to My Father and your Father, to My God and your God."

Jesus Appears on the Road to Emmaus

LATER that same day, two disciples were walking toward Emmaus. They were saddened about the events of the last few days, especially the death of Jesus.

Jesus appeared to them but they did not know Him. He explained the story of salvation to them and showed them that the Messiah had to undergo sufferings and death in order to enter into glory.

Then Jesus sat down to supper with them and they recognized Him as He broke the bread. Jesus disappeared. They hurried to Jerusalem to tell the other disciples.

Jesus Appears to the Disciples

ON the evening of the same day, the disciples were gathered in the Upper Room with the doors locked. Jesus came and stood in their midst. "Peace be with you," He said, and showed them His hands and feet.

"Peace be with you," He repeated. "As the Father sent Me, so I send you."

Then He breathed on them and said: "Receive the Holy Spirit. If you forgive people's sins, they are forgiven." By these words, Jesus gave to His first priests and their successors the power to forgive sins in the Sacrament of Penance.

Jesus Appears to Thomas

THOMAS, one of the Twelve Apostles, was not present when Jesus had come. The others told him how they had seen the Lord, but Thomas said: "Unless I see the marks of the nails and put my hand in His wounds, I will not believe."

A week later, Jesus appeared again to the Apostles. He called Thomas and told him to touch His wounds. Thomas said: "My Lord and my God!"

Jesus said: "You became a believer because you saw Me. Blessed are they who have not seen and have believed."

We do not see Jesus in the Mass and Holy Communion, but our faith tells us He is there as our Sacrifice and our Food.

Jesus Appears at the Seashore

ONE day when the disciples were fishing, Jesus appeared to them again, but they did not know Him. From shore, He told them to cast their nets on the right side of the ship, and they did so.

All night they had caught nothing, but this time they caught so many fish that they were unable to bring them ashore. John said to Peter: "It is the Lord." At once Peter jumped into the water and came ashore.

The others followed and they all ate together. Then Jesus told Peter to take care of His Church: "Feed My Sheep."

Jesus Sends the Disciples
to Teach the Faith

BEFORE leaving the disciples after His Resurrection, Jesus told them many things. He sent them out to preach the Good News to everyone.

He said: "Full authority has been given to Me, both in heaven and on earth. Go and make disciples of all nations. Baptize them in the Name of the Father and of the Son and of the Holy Spirit. Teach them to carry out everything I have commanded you. And know that I am with you always, until the end of the world."

Jesus is with us in His Church through the word of His Truth, and through His presence in the Holy Eucharist.

Jesus Ascends to Heaven

AFTER 40 days, Jesus led His disciples to a mountain and opened their minds to understand the Scriptures. He said: "It is written that the Messiah had to suffer and to rise again, and that repentance and forgiveness of sins had to be preached to all."

He told them that they were to be witnesses of these things. But they should wait for the coming of the Holy Spirit. As He blessed them, He went up to heaven.

Jesus is ever pleading for us as our Mediator with the Father and as the Eternal High Priest.

61

The Holy Spirit Comes Down
on Pentecost

WHILE the Apostles were still looking up into the sky after Jesus was taken up into heaven, two angels dressed in white came to them. "Men of Galilee," they said, "why do you stand here looking at the sky? This Jesus Who has been taken away from you up to heaven will come back in the same way that you saw Him go."

The Apostles knelt down and worshiped God. Then they turned back to Jerusalem with great joy, to the upper room where they lived together and prayed. Jesus had told them: "Stay in the city until you are clothed with power from on high. You will receive power when the Holy Spirit comes upon you. You are to be My witnesses in the whole world."

Ten days later, on Pentecost Sunday, the disciples were with our Lady. Suddenly they heard a sound from heaven like the noise of a great wind.

They saw tongues of fire, and they were filled with the Holy Spirit. They began to praise God, and to tell all the people how good God is and how wonderful are all His works. The sending of the Holy Spirit is the birthday of the Catholic Church which Jesus founded.

Jesus, Our King, Helps Us from Heaven

JESUS said to Pilate: "My Kingdom does not belong to this world. The reason I was born, the reason why I came into the world, is to speak about the truth. Whoever belongs to the truth, listens to Me."

If we want to have Christ for our King we must try to please Him always. We must let Jesus Christ live in us, filling our minds with His truths and our hearts with His love. We must belong to Him entirely, especially through Holy Communion and prayer.

Let us pray that all people will belong to His Kingdom.

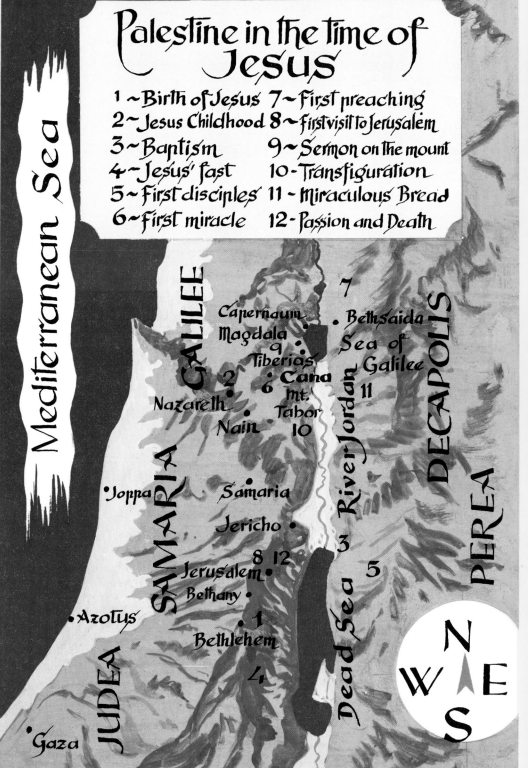